Date: 9/14/15

Dachshunds

Stephanie Finne

Checkerboard
Library

An Imprint of Abdo Publishing
www.abdopublishing.com

www.abdopublishing.com

Published by Abdo Publishing, a division of ABDO, PO Box 398166, Minneapolis, MN 55439.
Copyright © 2015 by Abdo Consulting Group, Inc. International copyrights reserved in all
countries. No part of this book may be reproduced in any form without written permission from
the publisher. Checkerboard Library™ is a trademark and logo of Abdo Publishing.

Printed in the United States of America, North Mankato, Minnesota.
102014
012015

Cover Photo: iStockphoto
Interior Photos: Gerard Lacz/FLPA/Minden Pictures p. 11; Glow Images pp. 5, 12–13, 19, 21;
    iStockphoto pp. 1, 7, 8–9, 16, 16–17

Series Coordinator: Tamara L. Britton
Editors: Megan M. Gunderson, Bridget O'Brien
Production: Jillian O'Brien

Library of Congress Cataloging-in-Publication Data

Finne, Stephanie, author.
  Dachshunds / Stephanie Finne.
      pages cm. -- (Dogs)
  Audience: Ages 8-12.
  Includes index.
  ISBN 978-1-62403-674-3
1. Dachshunds--Juvenile literature. I. Title.
  SF429.D25F56 2015
  636.753'8--dc23
                        2014025407

Contents

The Dog Family

Dogs and humans have worked as a team for more than 12,000 years. Scientists believe dogs evolved from the gray wolf. These wolves were great hunters. Humans wanted to use those skills to make their own hunts more successful.

Humans soon tamed wolves and began to **breed** them. The pups bred from these wolves were the first dogs. So like wolves, dogs belong to the family **Canidae**.

Over time, humans developed a wide variety of dog breeds to do different jobs. Today, there are more than 400 breeds! Some are herding dogs. Others are loyal companions. Dachshunds were bred to hunt.

The dachshund

Dachshunds

The first dachshunds lived in Germany. The dogs were named after their skill of badger hunting. In German, *dachs* means "badger" and *hund* means "dog."

In the 1600s, foresters wanted short, strong dogs to hunt rabbits, foxes, badgers, and boars. The dogs had to be able to crawl through small spaces. They had to bark loud enough when underground to let hunters know where their prey was located.

German and English **immigrants** brought dachshunds to America. In 1884, the **American Kennel Club (AKC)** was formed. Dachshunds appeared in several AKC shows. But, the **breed** wasn't registered with the AKC until 1885. In 1895, the Dachshund Club of America was formed.

Since then, the **breed** has won awards in three of the eight **AKC** groups! Dachshunds first appeared in the working and sporting groups, but found their place in the hound group in 1931. More important, dachshunds have won the hearts of pet owners everywhere!

In 2013, dachshunds were the AKC's tenth most popular breed!

What They're Like

Dachshunds are very clever. They were **bred** to think for themselves while hunting. This can make them stubborn. They are determined to follow their noses, even if it means digging under the fence to follow a scent.

Dachshunds are very sweet to their owners. They are loyal companions, choosing one special family member as theirs. They are wonderful playmates to children in their family.

Dachshunds have many nicknames because of their shape. They are called hot dogs, wiener dogs, and slinky dogs.

Dachshunds will protect their humans from any threat. So, these lively dogs bark a lot. They bark at falling leaves, passing cars, and intruders. If not **socialized**, these dogs will bark and growl at neighbors or even houseguests.

Coat and Color

There are three types of coats for the lovable dachshund. They are smooth, longhair, and wirehair.

Smooth dachshunds have glossy hair. The coat is short all over, including on the tail. Smooth-coated dachshunds need weekly brushing.

The outer coat of the longhaired dachshund is glossy and wavy. The coat on the neck, chest, ears, tail, and abdomen is longer. Longhaired dachshunds need to be brushed twice a week to avoid tangles.

The wirehaired variety has a soft **undercoat**. The outer coat is short, hard, and wiry. The wirehair coat should be **hand stripped**. This will keep the hard, protective feel.

These three coats can be a variety of colors. They can be solid colors from cream to deep red. Dachshunds can also be two colors, combining black,

The smooth, wirehaired, and longhaired coat types

chocolate, or fawn with either tan or cream. Another
color is wild boar, which means the hair is **banded**.
Dachshunds can also be **merle**, **brindle**, or **sable**.

Size

Dachshunds come in many colors. But, this **breed** comes in just two sizes. These are standard and miniature.

Standard dachshunds are eight to nine inches (20 to 23 cm) tall. They must weigh more than 11 pounds (5 kg). On average, they weigh 16 to 32 pounds (7 to 15 kg). Miniature dachshunds weigh less than 11 pounds (5 kg). They are just five to six inches (13 to 15 cm) tall.

Dachshunds are short! Their short legs keep them close to the ground. Dachshunds were bred to have long, muscular

bodies. They have a deep chest and a long back. The tail is long and straight off the back.

The dachshund's head is tapered from the ears to the **muzzle**. Its rounded ears are set high on the head and hang down. Its medium, almond-shaped eyes are very dark. These features give the dachshund a keen, alert expression.

A dachshund's size depended on the animals it tracked. Miniature dogs hunted rabbits, while standard dogs hunted badgers and foxes.

13

Care

Dachshunds may be small, but most have a lot of energy in those little bodies! They were **bred** to be hunters, so they need exercise. Two walks a day should be enough.

Like all dogs, this breed requires regular checkups with a veterinarian. The vet will perform an exam and provide **vaccines**. He or she can **spay** or **neuter** dogs that will not be bred.

Dachshunds like to have fun. They want to be included in activities and chores. But they are also independent. They think for themselves, so they can be difficult to train.

The most important thing you can give your dachshund is love. These dogs do not like to be separated from their humans. If your dog is going to

Dachshunds need an occasional bath, along with weekly ear cleaning and nail trimming.

be alone for long periods of time, it is a good idea to keep it entertained. A dachshund should have toys to play with or another dog to keep it company.

Feeding

Dachshunds don't just love attention. They also love to eat! That means they easily become overweight.

It is important to watch what and how much dachshunds eat. Your vet may suggest a small morning meal and a larger evening meal for adult dachshunds. Puppies should eat four times a day.

All dogs need a balanced diet to be healthy. This must include **protein**. Choose a food that is labeled "complete and balanced."

This means it contains all the **nutrients** your dog needs.

There are different types of dog food. Dry foods help clean your dog's teeth. Semimoist foods are softer and do not need to be refrigerated. Canned foods are moist, but they spoil quickly.

Dog treats can also be a part of your dog's day. Because this **breed** loves food, treats are a good training tool. But be careful not to give too many.

Always provide your dog with fresh water.

Things They Need

Besides healthy food, your dachshund will need some additional things. Start with food and water dishes. Bowls with rubber on the bottom are less likely to slide around. Your dachshund should also have a crate. This will be a comfortable den for your pet.

All dogs need to wear a collar with license and identification tags. You will need a leash to walk your dog. A vet can also insert a **microchip** into your new pet. This chip will help identify your pet if it escapes or gets lost.

You will need toys to entertain your new friend. Dogs enjoy playing with balls, ropes, and chew toys. Staying busy keeps a dog out of trouble!

Keeping your clever dachshund busy will keep it out of trouble.

Puppies

A female dog is **pregnant** for about 63 days. Having puppies is called whelping. The number of puppies in a **litter** depends on the size of the dachshund.

All puppies are born blind, deaf, and unable to walk. A puppy's eyes open after two weeks. After another two weeks it can see, hear, and play.

At eight weeks old, a puppy is ready to leave its mother. A good **breeder** makes sure the puppy is healthy and has its shots. So, find a reputable breeder to choose your new puppy. Then, begin basic training right away.

It is important to **socialize** your dachshund. Introduce your new family member to other people and experiences. This will help it be a good companion for the next 12 to 14 years.

Standard dachshunds have three to eight puppies in a litter. Miniatures have three to four puppies.

Glossary

American Kennel Club (AKC) - an organization that studies and promotes interest in purebred dogs.

banded - having or marked by narrow strips of different color.

breed - a group of animals sharing the same ancestors and appearance. A breeder is a person who raises animals. Raising animals is often called breeding them.

brindle - having dark streaks or spots on a gray, tan, or tawny background.

Canidae (KAN-uh-dee) - the scientific Latin name for the dog family. Members of this family are called canids. They include wolves, jackals, foxes, coyotes, and domestic dogs.

hand strip - a grooming style in which dead hair is pulled out of a dog's coat by hand or with a stripping knife.

immigrant - a person who enters another country to live.

litter - all of the puppies born at one time to a mother dog.

merle - having dark patches of color on a lighter background.

microchip - an electronic circuit placed under an animal's skin. A microchip contains identifying information that can be read by a scanner.

muzzle - an animal's nose and jaws.

neuter (NOO-tuhr) - to remove a male animal's reproductive glands.

nutrient - a substance found in food and used in the body. It promotes growth, maintenance, and repair.

pregnant - having one or more babies growing within the body.

protein - a substance which provides energy to the body and serves as a major class of foods for animals. Foods high in protein include cheese, eggs, fish, meat, and milk.

sable - having black-tipped hairs on a silver, gold, gray, fawn, or brown background.

socialize - to adapt an animal to behaving properly around people or other animals in various settings.

spay - to remove a female animal's reproductive organs.

undercoat - short hair or fur partly covered by longer protective fur.

vaccine (vak-SEEN) - a shot given to prevent illness or disease.

Websites

To learn more about Dogs, visit **booklinks.abdopublishing.com**. These links are routinely monitored and updated to provide the most current information available.

Index